BUD TAKE THE WHEEL,
I FEEL A SONG COMING ON

Clara Brennan

BUD TAKE THE WHEEL, I FEEL A SONG COMING ON

OBERON BOOKS
LONDON

WWW.OBERONBOOKS.COM

First published in 2011 by Oberon Books Ltd
521 Caledonian Road, London N7 9RH
Tel: +44 (0.) 20 7607 3637 / Fax: +44 (0.) 20 7607 3629
e-mail: info@oberonbooks.com
www.oberonbooks.com

A catalogue record for this book is available from the British
Library.

ISBN: 978-1-84943-076-0

Cover design by Tom Sebright

In memory of Clare Hope.

Bud Take The Wheel, I Feel A Song Coming On by Clara Brennan received its World Premiere at The Underbelly, on 5th August 2010, as part of the Edinburgh Fringe Festival 2010, produced by Reclaim Productions and SPL.

Cast (in order of appearance)

Frances, Yvonne Martin
Liam, Tim Dewberry
Paula, Anna Kirke
Bud, Roger Ringrose
Christian, Gunnar Cauthery

Director, Hannah Price
Designer, Carla Goodman
Costume Assistant, Ed Parry
Sound Designer, Steve Brown
Lighting Designer, Martin McLachlan
Stage Manager, Surenee Chan Somchit
Stage Manager, Laura Elliot
Graphic Design, Tom Sebright
PR, Elin Morgan at Prospero
Producer, Katie Harper and Hannah Price
Production Manager, Jennifer Pearce
Production Assistant, Laura Haigh

Reclaim Productions and SPL would like to thank the following for their kind assistance *(in alphabetical order)*: Ed Bartlam, Caitlin Albery Beaven, Marina Dixon, David Michel, Anne and Urquhart Neilson, Craig Neilson, Annie and Richard Price, Jamie Rocha Allan, Fiona Stewart, Theatre 503, The Shaw Theatre.

For Reclaim:
Artistic Director, Hannah Price
Artistic Associate, Jamie Rocha Allan

For SPL:
Producer, Adam Speers
Producer, Aron Rollin

Characters

BRIAN 'BUD' CUDDEN
late fifties

PAULA CUDDEN
late fifties

CHRISTIAN CUDDEN
Their son, late twenties

FRANCES CUDDEN
Their daughter, sweet sixteen

LIAM MULLEN
Bud's apprentice, early thirties

The present.
An old mill town
five miles from everything else.

The family has its regional accent,
aside from Christian, who has lost his,
and Frances, who is working on it.

ONE

Above –

The roof of a thatched cottage on the outskirts of a village. A ladder rests against the eaves. On top of the ridge, besides the dining-room chimneystack, sit FRANCES and LIAM. He has stretched out a cut-off of blue tarpaulin beneath them. He smokes a cigarette and holds an empty beer can between his knees.

FRANCES: Where's your ash going?

LIAM: In here.

He gestures to his beer can.

FRANCES: You going to say something?

LIAM: I'm thinking, woman! I *am* thinking!

FRANCES: Jesus it's like watching a kettle boil with no water in it.

LIAM: Aghh, stop talking!

FRANCES: No, you take your time Liam, take your time. We've got a good seven months. Think of it like a battle scenario: *(Imitates radio crackle.)* "CCrrzzzckkzz May day, may day, we've got an embryo situation. The enemy is within! Foxtrot, Uniform, Charlie, Kilo! Over-and-out!"

He turns to look at her.

LIAM: I'm thinking 'what's there to think about?'

FRANCES: Oh perfect!

LIAM: I'm thinking there's nothing to think about, is there? I mean. In that you've got a future – And I'm thirty-two. I've got no prospects besides being apprenticed now. I've got my kit bag and a dog and no savings, and I'm still working things out –

FRANCES: You've got transferable skills.

LIAM: Don't start.

FRANCES: Install broadband; lay cable, anything – telecoms!

LIAM: I don't want anything to do with it.

FRANCES: You didn't kill anyone.

LIAM: Didn't I?

FRANCES: Give me a drag.

He puffs on the cigarette. He hands it to FRANCES.

LIAM: What does it matter anyway; he's going to fucking kill me!

FRANCES: It's Mum you've got to watch out for. Stab you through the heart with a fucking dibber.

LIAM: I deserve it.

FRANCES: Oh don't be so macabre.

LIAM: I don't know what that means.

FRANCES: It means you're guilt personified.

LIAM: You don't know anything about it!

FRANCES: Don't get pissy with *me!*

LIAM: I'm not pissy with you – Frances – I'm not.

FRANCES: I've eaten nothing but crystallized bloody ginger for the past week trying to stop myself puking, and all you care about's his bloody business!

LIAM: I want to be loyal, if anything/

FRANCES: Oh nice, nice. Well staying here's not loyalty; it's a bloody penance!

They stare at each other for a moment in comprehending horror.

FRANCES: So it's finished?

LIAM: What?

FRANCES: This. *(She gestures to the roof.)*

LIAM: Tomorrow they move in. Look, Fran –

FRANCES: Got kids?

LIAM: Three I think your Dad said.

FRANCES: Weekenders.

LIAM: Looks like.

FRANCES: Huh.

She looks down at the thatch.

They first put this on in the fourteenth century. Imagine that.

LIAM: I can't.

FRANCES: Walls of wattle and daub.

FRANCES: My big brother's back the day after tomorrow.

LIAM: Beat me up too will he?

FRANCES: Who Christian? No. No.

He's obscenely tolerant.

LIAM: He's – ?

FRANCES: I haven't seen him in eight years.

LIAM: When you planning on telling them?

FRANCES: I don't know/

LIAM: I need to know/

FRANCES: Why? So you can hit the road?

I'm not stopping you.

LIAM: What you on about?

FRANCES: I can deal with it. *(She looks at him.)*

I'm going to go to university and form a band and get a First.

LIAM: Then you've decided, then?

FRANCES: Suppose I have.

LIAM: It's just – if you're not having it then – there might be no reason/

FRANCES: What?

LIAM: – Getting everyone upset.

FRANCES: *(Exploding.)* How'm I going to deal with it without them knowing?

LIAM: I can – drive you. Wherever it is – you go.

She starts to edge towards the ladder.

FRANCES: Oh very good! *Very* good Liam!

LIAM: Hang on – Fran, wait up/

FRANCES: You're a fucking chump/

LIAM: Let me go down first and hold the ladder/

FRANCES: Fuck off you will. Knock me off's more likely!

FRANCES reaches the ladder and starts to climb down. LIAM leans towards the edge.

LIAM: I can give you a lift/

FRANCES: Best not, eh Liam?

LIAM: Say I picked you up/

FRANCES: I picked *you* up! Jesus fucking Christ Liam! *(She mockingly addresses the heavens.)* How a prick with no balls got me up the duff, Lord *only knows!*

(She climbs down the ladder.)

I want this parasite ripped out of me!

LIAM sighs audibly. He puts the cigarette butt in the beer can and swishes it round. He checks his jacket pockets for another cigarette.

TWO

Two hours later.

The low-ceilinged living room of a converted terrace of worker's cottages – two two-up two-down cottages, now united, comprise the entire house. This room was the ground floor of one cottage, with a front door opening onto it, and another door to the hallway and the rest of the house. One window at the front, and one at the back looking onto the garden provide little natural light. A cluster of boots lined up beside the front door stand on yellowed newspaper. A battered settee is covered with various blanket throws. A dining table is pushed against the back window and is covered with newspaper, planting trays, plant pots, and a toolbox full of gardening tools. A television stands in the corner. It is not switched on. PAULA CUDDEN is a slim-woman-with-an-incongruous-rounded-stomach-that-never-flattened-due-to-the-death-of-stillborn-twins-at-

eight-months. She developed a stoop, it is an old stoop. She is tenderly re-potting a very fertile money tree: its offspring are already in their new pots. Her daughter FRANCES sits on the settee reading a guide book of guitar chords. FRANCES tends to speak to her only when spoken to, and as a result PAULA tends to converse only in questions.

PAULA: Well I don't use it anymore so you might as well get it down and make use of it, hey?

FRANCES: Mm.

PAULA: No use just reading about chords, is there?

FRANCES: No.

PAULA: I should love you to have it. We'll get it out the loft?

Into this happy scene comes BUD CUDDEN. He enters through the front door with gusto. FRANCES never looks up from her book. PAULA moves to greet him, but stops dead:

PAULA: Good God Alive. What are you wearing?

BUD: It's my wedding suit.

PAULA: I see that.

BUD: Shoes a bit tight. Is it possible my feet grew?

PAULA: Yeah, in proportion. Where've you/ *(Smelling his breath.)* You've been at the pub.

BUD: I had a half day. Don't start/

PAULA: Good God – you've been *out* out in that? What on earth for? Do you see what your father's wearing?

FRANCES looks at her mother briefly.

BUD: I put on my funeral one, but there's the burn hole in the thigh.

PAULA: Somebody die?

BUD: *(Pointedly.)* Not yet.

PAULA: Did you finish the job or no?

BUD: They're moving in tomorrow.

PAULA: You'll have to invoice sharpish/

BUD: Yes boss.

PAULA: Don't leave it a week, I'm serious, we need this/

BUD: All right! I know it! I know it! Do you have to always bollock-on about money, Paula!

PAULA: Don't swear – in front of Frances.

They both regard their daughter.

PAULA: Where've you been that wants a suit?

BUD: I'm near telling you, woman. You're looking at an *elect* member of the Parish Council.

PAULA: The what?

BUD: They think I've got some good insights. Being a *local* master craftsman, and having a son who's a –

PAULA: Don't say it/

BUD: I wasn't going to say *poof* – a son who happens to be the developer/

PAULA: Oh Christ, Bud/

BUD: What?

PAULA: This is Christian's project, his career/

BUD: One young upstart gets his first big contract, and for what, forty men out of a job/

PAULA: It's high time that place was *developed/*

BUD: And where are they now? Eh? Six years on? I've just spent an hour with them at *The Wheatsheaf!* I'm ashamed/

PAULA: How did you get on the Council?

BUD: *(Sheepish.)* I won't lie to you. I've offered to over-coat the rectory.

PAULA: For free?

He shrugs. Her eyes glance to the heavens. About to erupt:

BUD: Before you start/

PAULA: For free/

BUD: Trouble with you Paula is, you've not got a bone, of generosity in your body –

PAULA: Me? Generosity!

BUD: Always twisting things –

PAULA: Oh I'm twisting things? I can't see you going to all this trouble if it wasn't your own son's name on the site notice!/

BUD: It's my name too! In case you forgot.

PAULA: What does that mean?

BUD: Just –

PAULA: What –

BUD: There's no harm in a local man having his say – the mill means a lot to the parish/

PAULA: The parish. *(She scoffs.)*

BUD: And I'd like to see any development handled with respect – for the people who actually live here!

PAULA: Christian grew up here/

BUD: Hasn't lived here in eight years!

PAULA: He's coming home tomorrow. He has the meeting on Monday/

BUD: So have I now!

PAULA: Yeah, and the minute he's headed back you try to what? Get on the bloody council; you're trying to prevent our son from staying here, after all these years? You *promised!*/

BUD: We've got Liam here now. We've rented his room to Liam!

PAULA: We've said he'll have the sofa! Oh my *god* if you drive him off again/

BUD: Well that's up to him. He's got a mind of his own hasn't he?/

PAULA: I'd give up my own bed if you weren't always lumped in it! Or we can put them in there together, separate the bunk/

BUD: We'll not put them together, Paula.

PAULA: I'm warning you Bud. He's our *son* –

BUD: *(Pointedly.)* But he's not *at home* with the rest of the family.

She pauses, considers this an insult.

A tiny screaming noise is heard.

FRANCES turns her head to the garden.

PAULA: Did you hear that?

BUD: What?

PAULA: *(To FRANCES.)* Did *you* hear that?

Their attention turns to their daughter. She opens her mouth to answer, but reconsiders and closes it again. She shakes her head at her Mother.

I thought I heard a tiny – scream.

BUD: Where?

PAULA: Not sure.

BUD: Tiny scream! That'd be tinnitus setting in, like your mother.

PAULA: Some sort of squeak, I heard.

BUD: If it's mice it'll be all the biscuits down the back of that settee.

They look to their daughter again. PAULA frowns.

PAULA: I definitely heard something.

BUD: Maybe it was the church bells.

PAULA: When've you ever heard the church bells?

BUD: What'd you mean, 'when have I ever heard the bells?'

PAULA: Shall I put the telly on now love?

BUD: Can't hear anything but bloody bells.

FRANCES doesn't look up. She shrugs.

BUD: Nose stuck in a book. You want to be outside in the holidays.

PAULA: She's been out there hurling the pondweeds on the bonfire.

BUD: You watched her?/

PAULA: Oh she was fine! It hardly burns for all that scum.

They observe their daughter.

PAULA: I've seen a frog already. It worried me when I saw it, how green it was. Like they've camouflaged with the algae. Least someone finally got to cleaning it. One of your old work boots, Liam found in there. One of your boots.

BUD: I've got to have a pee. I've a whole urn of tea inside me.

PAULA: And a brewery I don't doubt.

BUD: I watched the darts after. *(He moves towards the hall door. She starts to follow him.)*

PAULA: I'll need you to get up in the loft/

BUD: What for now?

PAULA: If you're sober enough to get on a ladder/

BUD: *(Steadily.)* Paula.

PAULA: *(Steadily.)* Frances is going to have my old guitar.

BUD: Oh that's good! That's good, Frances! *(To Paula.)* You still got it?

PAULA: Course I've still got it.

FRANCES frowns. She continues to study the book.

PAULA: Christian's getting to the station at nine tomorrow morning.

BUD: Well some of us have to work weekends; I'll be long gone –

He goes out.

She follows him out.

PAULA: No, he'll arrive in a taxi. He gets expenses. Honestly, the girth of those bell bottoms! I could have taken them in. I would have taken them in if I'd known you were going to squeeze yourself into that.

FRANCES frowns. She continues to study the book.

THREE

The following day. Late afternoon.

PAULA sits at the dining table in front of her son's laptop. She is peering closely at the screen. Immaculately suited, CHRISTIAN is standing behind her in the shadows, looking over her shoulder through the window to the back garden. An acoustic guitar lies on the sofa, an expensive piece of luggage beside it.

PAULA: Where's 'delete'? Christian? *(She turns to appraise him.)*

CHRISTIAN: *(He leans over, peers and points.)* – There.

PAULA: Although I will say, I was leaving a note for your father when I went shopping last week and I looked down and I'd written half of it in shorthand! Some things I haven't lost. Although if I'd had to learn on one of these things I would have never gotten out of the pool. You want a snack? A sandwich?

CHRISTIAN: No. I'm fine, thank you.

PAULA: You ought to have something, you ate hardly any lunch. *(She turns to look at him.)*

You've taken after your Granddad's side. Your Granddad Ward, that is. Fair and slim like my lot – You almost look like him, you do. Watching you walk in, you had this very – elegant way. A strong but very elegant – gait, I suppose.

CHRISTIAN: Oh dear, did I mince?

PAULA: *No!* No I'm saying like my old Dad was – And it's your hands, too, you know. Way your hands move when you're walking. You move like him. Where's that picture of him holding the bike in India? You'll see what I mean, his hands – it's on the hall wall –

PAULA stands.

CHRISTIAN: I've missed you.

They watch each other uncertainly.

PAULA: And your skin cleared up – didn't it? After all that, do you remember? Agonising over the acne, you called it that, now I always said it wasn't, it was just normal teenage pores, and it was never all over like some of your friends, poor things, that Mark boy, oh; and you've not got that awful pitted skin like some poor people do, the scarring. Little dimples, pitted, like an orange. Have you?

CHRISTIAN: No, I suppose not.

PAULA: No. Smooth, you've got lovely skin, you have.

CHRISTIAN: Thank you for this.

PAULA: Oh no! I've enjoyed this, bit of dictation! I never really got to use my typing –

CHRISTIAN: You never did go back to work.

PAULA: No. *(She looks down, briefly, at her stomach.)*

CHRISTIAN: No.

PAULA: I could have, between the twins and Frances.

CHRISTIAN: But you were ill.

PAULA: Well I don't know, it wasn't me that –

They'd be twenty.

Imagine.

CHRISTIAN: Twenty.

PAULA: Imagine.

You never told me what you did?

CHRISTIAN: When?

PAULA: Your birthday. This year.

CHRISTIAN: Oh nothing much. Had dinner with friends.

PAULA: Oh that's nice. I tried calling/

CHRISTIAN: Yeah.

PAULA: You know, it feels like you've never been away!

CHRISTIAN: Does it?

PAULA: Doesn't it?

CHRISTIAN: Mum –

PAULA: Have I changed so much?

CHRISTIAN: No. No you haven't changed.

PAULA: And your father doesn't change.

CHRISTIAN: No?

PAULA: He looks good for his age. Bit heavier, but that's the quitting smoking.

CHRISTIAN: God, has he?

PAULA: He was like a bear with a sore head for a few months, and he definitely likes his sweets more now.

CHRISTIAN: When did he quit?

PAULA: Oh, not long after you left for university.

A look between them. They smile.

CHRISTIAN: What's he working on now?

PAULA: Oh, he's got a great job on. A young city couple bought themselves a derelict cottage on the corner at Keynston Bridge? Hasn't been habitable for years, it's been quite a pet project for him, and finally when he gets up there to give it an over-coat – it's all decayed, and then he notices: it's blackened where it touches the rafters!

CHRISTIAN: Ah – !

PAULA: Yes – !

CHRISTIAN: – Sorry – is that a good thing?

PAULA: He stripped it down to the oldest thatch, and it's smoke blackened: so old it pre-dates the use of chimneys! And he gets on the phone, god knows how he knows these blokes, but they turn up and it's – what is it – the Archaeo-Botany society or something, and they're all climbing-all-over-him-in-little-white-gloves, talking-about-carbon-dating-and-this,-and-that, and later they say it's been there since the fourteenth century! They were congratulating him on the Discovery!

So work halted for a while there, and once it was all, I don't know, recorded, he got the go ahead, so he's doing the finishing touches now.

CHRISTIAN: Ah yes, his little thatch pheasants on the ridge.

PAULA: Why'd you always have to rib him about those? What'd you expect him to put up there? Lions?

CHRISTIAN: Sorry, Mum.

PAULA: They're his signature.

A Pause.

She looks at him searchingly.

PAULA: You could still pass for eighteen.

He laughs.

PAULA: Eight, years.

CHRISTIAN: Mum. We've been over this.

PAULA: How long can you stay? Do you think?

CHRISTIAN: We'll see. My meeting's tomorrow.

PAULA: But this one's the best yet, I mean it's much more – hang on, I've just twigged – you're putting thatches down there?

CHRISTIAN: Well, it's not the vernacular for Newtown/

PAULA: It's slate and tile/

CHRISTIAN: But it complements aspects of the main village, as a whole.

PAULA: You've done this for your father? Oh Christian, that's a good gesture! Do you think he'd get the contract? Putting thatches down there/

CHRISTIAN: I should be able to swing it.

PAULA: So what's that – a pair of semi-detached, two detached cottages/

CHRISTIAN: *(Hopefully.)* Would he see it as charity?

PAULA: He's not so proud, Christian. Not any more.

She gets up and stretches.

PAULA: He's had trouble getting his nitches locally. He has to drive to the next county to get wheat that hasn't been combined. When you think how it used to be – now you're paying them over the odds for special threshing. Your Dad says it's "Man versus Machine from here on", he acts like it happened over night! They're shutting the Dry Quarry next year. More drinking buddies for your father

She follows his gaze out the window to the back garden.

more ear-ache for me.

CHRISTIAN: Where's Fran going?

PAULA: I asked her to take him for a walk.

CHRISTIAN: It was a shock to see a dog run out, the taxi nearly had him. I thought *you'd* gotten a dog! And I'd finally been replaced.

PAULA: He's/not ours

CHRISTIAN: He belongs to this lodger?

PAULA: Liam, yes. Though I've found myself in the aisles fretting over which small bite mixer to get him. Don't get too quick with him though, he's not got a lot going on up here. Likes Frances though.

CHRISTIAN: She's grown.

PAULA: Sixteen – going on twenty-five. You got my letters.

CHRISTIAN: I meant to reply/

PAULA: Maybe she'll be a bit more talkative with you here. Maybe – you'll talk to her?

CHRISTIAN: Course I will, Mum.

She smiles at him sadly.

PAULA: And did you see my pond?

CHRISTIAN: Oh, no –

PAULA: Liam's cleared it and my frogs are back. Two I saw this morning, great big buggers!

CHRISTIAN: Where did Dad find him?

PAULA: Oh he found your father. He tapped on his ladder one day, and he says: 'There's not many of you blokes around anymore', and your Dad looked down and laughed, cos someone says that to him nearly every day, don't they? And they got chatting, and all of a sudden he's apprenticed. Dog sleeps outside though, that was my only request.

CHRISTIAN: And he's in my room.

PAULA: I know – I never thought about renting it, ever, Christian, I mean, the thought of having a stranger! But he's a lovely boy, Christian, ex-squaddie but he's got such a head for heights. And seeing as they work together anyways; and your Dad can't pay him much, especially when it's wet; and you – being in the city/

CHRISTIAN: If I'd known/

PAULA: It wouldn't hurt, would it, to sleep down here?

CHRISTIAN: We'll see/

PAULA: Oh I knew you'd be put out, I said to your Dad, I said, we could separate the bunk beds and squeeze you in there with Liam, but he said it'd never do, two grown men/

He raises his eyebrows at her.

(Covering.) It's such a small room there with the ceiling sloped/

CHRISTIAN: I'll be all right down here.

PAULA: You will? Frances offered you her room, she's like me – oh Christian, we're both jumping around like bloody Jack Russells now you're back. We – want you to be comfortable, to stay –

CHRISTIAN: I'll be fine. Honestly.

PAULA: Alright – it can be like all those times either of you was ill and we'd bring your bedding down – *(She is visibly upset.)*

CHRISTIAN: Don't get upset please, Mum/

PAULA: Eight years –

CHRISTIAN: I know/

PAULA: And I'm treading on eggshells, I am, I'm trying not to say – anything to drive you off.

CHRISTIAN: I don't want there to be eggshells, I want us to express/

PAULA: I was convinced, you'd come back after your graduation/

CHRISTIAN: You're still upset about that/

PAULA: You get those posed portraits done of you in your gown, with the – scroll – if I'd been there, I probably would have bullied you into having one taken, you know what I'm like –

CHRISTIAN: But I didn't go –

PAULA: I know, that's just it! You said not to get a ticket as you weren't going. You went away!

CHRISTIAN: I did a lot of thinking –

PAULA: Course you did, getting a First!

CHRISTIAN: Outside of studying, Mum. I had some counselling/

PAULA: God, why, what for?

CHRISTIAN: Just the campus therapist, just to get me through my finals. It was nothing.

PAULA: *(Quietly.)* It's my fault.

CHRISTIAN: It's not! No, god, I said I wouldn't lie: maybe it is! Maybe it is, do you really want to hear that? I still haven't figured it all out yet. And if truth be told I've had a therapist every bloody Thursday for the past three years/

PAULA: You've gotten cold.

CHRISTIAN: I've gotten angrier. Go on. Ask. Ask if it's a woman or a man I see.

PAULA: Why is it important, I don't want to know/

CHRISTIAN: I've had therapists of both genders. I always thought I blamed him, I did. But/

PAULA: You blame me.

CHRISTIAN: I feel self-made.

PAULA: How do you mean/

CHRISTIAN: Parents – should raise you, not knock you down, protect you, not/

PAULA: Yes, there it is – yes, it's for never leaving him/

CHRISTIAN: Never leaving him and taking us away, *me* away, yes. Never stepping in when he clouted me round the head, yes, never correcting him when he said I'd amount to nothing, yes! To nothing, Mum!

PAULA: It was the drink talking, he never meant it!

CHRISTIAN: But my darling what did you think you were *doing*? Preserving the family unit? I got the shit kicked out of me and it got worse when he found out, you made your choice/

PAULA: No/

CHRISTIAN: No – It's not safe here/

PAULA: No, he's changed, Christian he really has, not always at boiling point any more. And Christian – darlin', I stepped in. I did darlin'. Don't you remember it?

CHRISTIAN: *(Wearily.)* I would remember. You never stopped him, not once, too afraid.

PAULA: I was not afraid to step in let's get that bloody clear straight away! I stepped in and I've been paying for it ever since!

CHRISTIAN: What do you mean?

PAULA: Nothing. Back then, it wasn't so easy to leave a husband, just like it wasn't so easy to leave your own parent's house in the first place. Wasn't so easy for women. And all those hopes I had of singing, well, they weren't realistic.

CHRISTIAN: They were!

PAULA: I'm working-class and I've barely worked a day in my life. Don't you think that's funny? My sisters all envy me it, but you know it's not like we could ever really live on just your Dad's wage, and we're still – we're flat broke, pretending/

CHRISTIAN: Too fucking proud to let you go out to work – even when you felt better!

PAULA: In some respects, nowadays yes, he wants to live like – a business man, not have me go out to work just to help with the bills, it's a bit of pride/

CHRISTIAN: 'Help with the bills'? Mum, you could have had a *career*/

PAULA: It was important to your father that he had made it further than his own Dad.

CHRISTIAN: He's never left this bloody place!

PAULA: You know what I mean. Self-employed.

CHRISTIAN: Self-employment's not exactly the height of the social climb, Mum. Jesus, the class aspirations of a fucking thatcher ruined your life!

PAULA: It's more complicated than that, it really is.

CHRISTIAN: You had options.

PAULA: Yes and maybe I made the wrong choice, without realising I had a choice, I'm stupid!

CHRISTIAN: You are not!

PAULA: God, you and me, we were thick as thieves. I never thought you'd be the one to leave, even though everyone said you were so bright, and you are, so bright – but it was your sister always had her eyes on the door, even when she was crawling, and now look/

CHRISTIAN: She's a teenager now/

PAULA: Because she always listened to you – several times her friends from the school have phoned and she won't let me tell them she's here.

CHRISTIAN: It's the holidays/

PAULA: But she thinks she might not go back, and she's supposed to have decided about Sixth Form. And she had a Saturday job at the hairdressers but she stopped going and now I have to do my own colour – I colour my hair now – they phoned and asked me what happened to her and she just stopped going and didn't tell me! And I lied and said 'Oh she's got glandular fever!' First thing that came into my head!

CHRISTIAN: I'll talk to her.

PAULA: The truth is, Christian – she doesn't really talk to us.

CHRISTIAN: Well that's normal/

PAULA: It's not. It is not. Normal. Christian. Sometimes she answers me when I ask her something, but more often than not she just shakes her head at me. And – the thing is she really won't say a word to your Dad! I can't remember the last time she even said 'hello'! I told you about those bus stops? They couldn't prove it was her, but – the kids from the village are a rowdy lot. You'd think they didn't have homes to go to. And she – there was the time I came downstairs and she had the wood-burner open and she paused – staring right at me – and she chucked a tin of lighter fluid in there, we're lucky the chimney didn't catch! I covered it up, said it was my fault. She's so *angry* Christian! Could have roasted the place! *(She starts to cry.)* It's all a mess/ *(He hugs her.)*

CHRISTIAN: It's not –

PAULA: But I talk to you in my head! I keep walking past the mill to see if the site notice is still there cos I know it's your company. Your name's at the bottom. Kept wondering 'when's he going to come'? Or will he come, and not tell me he's here, five minutes away down the road?

CHRISTIAN: I'm sorry. I am.

PAULA: A mother can't live on bloody phone calls, she just can't.

CHRISTIAN: Well maybe if the bloody Council had given the fifth application a chance/

PAULA: They will now you're both/

CHRISTIAN: What?

PAULA: Oh, Lord. Ah, shit.

CHRISTIAN: What's he done?

PAULA: He's become – a member. They'll give it a proper read now/

CHRISTIAN: Since when? Why?

PAULA: Christian/

CHRISTIAN: Since when?

PAULA: Well, since yesterday/

CHRISTIAN: Oh that's handy/

PAULA: He wants to get involved!/Me and my big bloody mouth/

CHRISTIAN: First time for everything! /He can't help himself!

PAULA: Christian/

CHRISTIAN: It's been sat there empty for six years. They wanted me to oversee on the eco town we're building up North, but I fought to keep *this* project afloat. To think I wanted to give him the fucking thatching/

PAULA: A lot of his friends lost their jobs/

CHRISTIAN: So he *is* going to fuck this up!

PAULA: Don't be daft, Christian, he hasn't got any sway! You mustn't see it like that/

CHRISTIAN: How else am I supposed to see it? If it was anyone else, any other developer, he wouldn't give a toss!

PAULA: He just doesn't think it should have closed/

CHRISTIAN: There! You know he's not on that council to give me a boost. He's dead against it!

PAULA: So you see, he'd be against *any* developer/

CHRISTIAN: They were in trouble for years; they should have switched to recycled or something! I didn't close the bloody thing. Why is he so obsessed with that fucking mill?

PAULA: He wants to feel important, Christian. Next to you.

CHRISTIAN: Oh he's always made his superiority felt, alright.

PAULA winces at this implication.

This is a last ditched effort, Mum.

PAULA: Is it?

CHRISTIAN: I've run out of designs/

PAULA: Maybe this one'll be it.

She dries her eyes.

CHRISTIAN: Maybe.

Footsteps are heard outside.

PAULA: We'll see tomorrow –

BUD throws open the front door, he enters and stops short. LIAM follows him into the room. He closes the door behind them.

PAULA and CHRISTIAN stare at them. PAULA's eyes flicker to the floor and their boots. BUD and LIAM are covered, head to toe, in thick black soot. Their faces are smeared. Both men are utterly defeated.

PAULA: Bud?

CHRISTIAN: What happened?

BUD: There's been a fire –

BUD is exhausted, and steps forward to lean his hand on the arm of the settee.

LIAM: Keynston's Bridge – we were driving back and we heard the engines/

BUD: Fire brigade/

PAULA: Oh god/

BUD: Stopped and asked us how to get to the cottage/

LIAM: Just finished it!

PAULA: God No!

CHRISTIAN: *The* cottage?

BUD: We just come from there!

LIAM: We'd finished the roof and gone to the pub and in the time we were there, the damn thing caught/

BUD: Had a quick half to celebrate/

PAULA: Is anyone hurt?

BUD: The poor buggers only just moved in today!/

LIAM: Everyone got out, three kids, they're all fine/

BUD: They're s'posed – with a thatch like that –

LIAM: We went back with the firemen/

BUD: I told them they gotta give the fire service a six digit number – a grid reference/

LIAM: They'd been driving around and couldn't find the turning/

BUD: Lost!

LIAM: But you could see the smoke/

BUD: We'd only just left for Christ's sakes! They're supposed to tell them the best way for a truck to get to them, but there's no sign posts! Even with the SatNav, if you can't see the turning/

PAULA: That roof – ?

LIAM: It's gone.

PAULA: My god. I don't believe it, Bud –

BUD: You've gotta give them the grid reference for a site like that so's the brigade's got the route worked out! I told them, the Council shoulda told them! When you've gotta roof like that/

CHRISTIAN: Did they put the fire out?

BUD: Put it out?

CHRISTIAN: Yeah?

BUD: Put it out?! Thatch is made to throw off water!

LIAM: Can't just put a hose on it, see/

BUD: The firemen got up there to pull the netting off, only they couldn't see where the wire was/

LIAM: It was easy enough to spot/

BUD: I fitted the netting myself/

LIAM: So we got up there/

PAULA: Pulled it all down!

LIAM: Sliced it, it came off in a great roll but it caught flame at one end, and we tugged it off the roof and down we went with it.

PAULA: You alright? You're hurt!

BUD: Liam might have a burn there.

LIAM raises his arm.

LIAM: It's nothing, just caught my sleeve.

BUD: He wouldn't let the firemen look at it/

PAULA: I'll look at it/

LIAM: It's nothing, really Paula/

PAULA: Come on out and I'll get the kit down/

LIAM: Wasn't going to let them get an ambulance out here just for me/

PAULA: How did it start?

BUD: Who knows?

PAULA: They can't have had the chimney going?

BUD: No.

LIAM: Could have been electrical.

PAULA: Could have been the wiring? I just don't believe it, you just finish it, and the whole thing catches!

BUD: Enough! Jesus, there's no use bloody speculating, is there? They'll find the cause.

PAULA: It's not your fault though is it?

LIAM: No, no.

BUD: Doesn't matter whose fault it is, that's months of bollocking work!

PAULA: Did they pay you?

BUD: Agh, don't/

PAULA: Oh god!

BUD: I'd only just finished the job woman!

PAULA: And you'll start over, again?

BUD: I can't ask for paying twice! I don't know if I can ask them to pay for it now!

PAULA: But it's not your fault it burned! You said yourself, the grid reference, they would have been there a lot quicker if they'd known which track to take/

BUD: They're just a young family/

PAULA: But they're weekenders/

BUD: Not rolling in it though, are they?

LIAM: I don't think so, no/

PAULA: You can't do it again for free! And you need to be paid for the first time, it's not your fault!

BUD: Let it lie, woman! I wouldn't blame them if they abandoned the whole thing! The beams were swallowed too/

PAULA: Oh god, Bud/

BUD: Just leave it, leave it! We'll have to see.

PAULA: All that work, for nothing!

BUD: Just see to his arm, Paula! Deal with that!

She leads LIAM out by his good arm. LIAM, sensing the lost opportunity for introduction, gives CHRISTIAN a brief wave with the arm she leads as they exit –

PAULA: *(As she is leaving.)* Don't sit down, I'll grab a sheet – and run the bath –

BUD stands as he was, leaning on the sofa. He and CHRISTIAN cannot look at each other. They wait.

PAULA enters, tosses a sheet to CHRISTIAN. She gives him an encouraging look, and exits.

CHRISTIAN slowly unfolds the sheet. He spreads it on the settee. His father does not watch him. CHRISTIAN stands aside. BUD sits down ungraciously. Contrary to PAULA's description, her husband remains a man of insurmountable pride.

CHRISTIAN: Good to see you, Dad.

BUD makes what he thinks is an ironic face: i.e. 'Is it?' He closes his eyes and rubs his face. He leans back into the settee.

CHRISTIAN: I'm sorry about – the thatch.

BUD closes his eyes. Pause.

CHRISTIAN: I hear you got on the Council.

BUD: *(Eyes still closed.)* I was elected.

CHRISTIAN: Yesterday, I hear.

BUD: Uh-huh.

PAULA enters with two beers, in old glass pint mugs.

PAULA: He's going to live, I'm just going to dress his arm.

She smiles winningly at both men, gives them each a beer, pauses for a split-second at the door and exits.

CHRISTIAN: Cheers Mum.

(Cheerfully, with vigour, as if following the formulaic instigation of a fight.)

I always liked these glasses. Like a great glass fist.

BUD: Thought you'd come and deliver the next proposal yourself, did you?

CHRISTIAN: *(Brightly.):* Yes. Yes I did.

BUD opens his eyes and sits up.

BUD: Last one was a shambles. A gated street!

CHRISTIAN: Yes, it wasn't/

BUD: You've got no business with a private, security-gated street! Keep the knobs safe from the locals, would it?

CHRISTIAN: That wasn't all me, I'm just over-seeing/

BUD: Ay, course you are. Over-seeing.

CHRISTIAN: I mean, I'm no architect.

BUD: No, I daresay you're not.

CHRISTIAN: I'm sorry about the fire.

BUD makes another face: i.e., 'Not as sorry as I am'.

CHRISTIAN: Mum said you had specialists look at the roof –

BUD: Just leave it, damn it! What do you know about any of it!

CHRISTIAN: I was just interested, Dad/

BUD: Now he's interested! Doesn't show any interest in anything here until there's money to be made!

CHRISTIAN: You're talking about the Paper Mill.

BUD: You know I am.

CHRISTIAN: Dad, it was already long-closed when my company put in a proposal, the first one/

BUD: Ay, and how many more will it take, can't you get the message? The village doesn't want the mill developed! Nobody wants you here!

Pause.

CHRISTIAN: We should just leave it as it is?

BUD: Why not!

CHRISTIAN: I'm proposing to use the mill buildings now – keep some of the exterior, original features/

BUD: Oh that's generous of you.

CHRISTIAN: The development could be good for the village, bring some more young families in/

BUD: What planet are you on, Christian? Eh? Hasn't living in the big city knocked some sense into you, eh? I see which side you're on/

CHRISTIAN: Side?

BUD: The toffs! You turn the mill into cosy little dwellings, call it 'Ye Olde Paper Mill' and the only people that'll be able to afford them are the super-knobs from your city still affording weekend homes. And what about now? You in denial, boy? You wait now they're in again! You wait! This damn country'll be up shit creek – you're forgetting where you came from! You're forgetting what a bloody mess it was you were born into! You'll rebuild and they'll just be sitting empty, you'll have ruined something that should be left alone and you'll have wasted your firm's money, mark my words/

CHRISTIAN: Well Dad, I didn't know you were concerned/

BUD: Concerned! You haven't been a man in a bad economy! This is just the start! You're taking the piss out of your family doing this! Four years your name's been bandied about here – the "Cudden boy's returning home to tear down the mill, make a fortune off the backs of local men!" You know what? I'm ashamed your name's on that notice.

CHRISTIAN: It's your name too/

BUD: Ay, and your grandfather's! – he worked his whole god damn life in that mill and it means nothing to you! He'd be turning in his grave if he knew how you turned out!

CHRISTIAN: And how's that?

Beat.

BUD: You've got no sense of shame.

CHRISTIAN: Oh I do, I do!

BUD: You're no better than a vulture, all of you! Half the village out of work and most still on the dole. 'How's the thatching going, Bud?' 'Oh not so bad, can't complain'. 'Your son, he still working for that company in the city? Saw his name on the site notice, can it be your son Christian?' See that's where we differ, boy – you've joined the new-money-grabbers trying to put your own stamp on things, well your lot ain't got no stamp! You don't win awards for tearing things down! You ain't got a clue about restoration! You're just taking orders from the fat cats, the little guy they send out to push the paperwork!/

CHRISTIAN: Oh, *I'm* the little guy!

BUD: Sent you out here like a courier, to do their dirty work!

CHRISTIAN: Nothing fucking changes! You're so *fucking* small-minded/

BUD: Don't you dare in this house! Watch your language!

CHRISTIAN: No, fuck you!

BUD jumps up from the settee. CHRISTIAN jumps up too.

BUD: I won't have it in my house you jumped-up, smarmy little, bastard!

CHRISTIAN starts to laugh. He cannot help himself – it is an age-old reaction.

BUD: What's so funny? What's so bloody funny now, eh?

BUD stands poised ready to hit him, he grabs him by the shirt collar and lifts him viciously.

BUD: Stop laughing! Stop – Laughing like a bloody simpleton, you're deranged you are, you're not right! Coming back here to leech off these people!

PAULA enters the room.

A dog barks outside. The back door bangs.

PAULA: Bud! Leave him!

BUD tightens his grip. CHRISTIAN, though choked, is still laughing.

BUD: You – always – Smug little bastard, smug little – git!
Nobody wants you here! Stop laughing! You smug little
fuck!

PAULA: Let go, let *go* Bud!

CHRISTIAN: Watch the suit!

LIAM enters the living room from the hallway.

BUD: Watch the suit? Watch the suit? When you gonna learn?
I won't have it in my house! Wipe that fucking stupid grin
off your face or I'll do it for you!

PAULA: Bud! *No!*

LIAM moves forward.

*FRANCES enters the room through the front door, pushing past LIAM
and PAULA. BUD raises his fist –*

LIAM: Bud, mate!

FRANCES: No! Stop it! Stop it, Dad! *(She lunges between BUD
and CHRISTIAN, pulling them apart.)* Let him go! If you hit
him just once!

CHRISTIAN stops laughing. BUD releases him. He stares at FRANCES.

*PAULA covers her face. CHRISTIAN holds the edge of the settee to
regain balance. He catches sight of LIAM in the doorway. He smiles
jovially.*

FRANCES stands between BUD and CHRISTIAN.

BUD: You hear that?

(Recovering his breath.) That's the most she's spoken to me in
eight years. Called me 'Dad'.

*CHRISTIAN and FRANCES regard each other. CHRISTIAN's smile
disappears. FRANCES smiles at him heroically.*

Outside, a dog barks in the garden.

FOUR

Later that evening. Outside the Old Paper Mill in Newtown, beside the rapid flowing river. They stand against the mesh fencing at the perimeter of the site. CHRISTIAN smokes cigarette after cigarette. FRANCES twirls happily around him.

CHRISTIAN: 'Epic Win'?

FRANCES: Yeah and you say, like, 'Epic Fail' when something's shit.

CHRISTIAN: Right/

FRANCES: Like – last summer I went to an 'Epic Win' party in a field out by White Farm with my mates. We camped. Some of them had just gotten back from this trip to Barcelona, my art teacher organised it. But I couldn't go – which was an Epic Fail. I'm the only one that even had a job – shampoos and sets at fucking *Snips*, that lame-ass hairdressers next to Abbey National? I fucking *hated* it and I still didn't have enough to go, pay for the bed and board and the flights. But I was the only one who knew who Antoni Gaudí was. I mean, Christie, that school's still a fucking shit-hole! You know the director of the Architecture College Gaudí went to, said once: "I don't know if we've given the degree to a genius or to a lunatic. Time will give the answer". I thought that was brilliant, you know – half my teachers hate me and half of them think the sun like, shines out of my arse. You were the same, I remember. So in 1926, he, Gaudí, goes for a little walkabout like all days, and gets run over by a streetcar. He had no ID on him, and his clothes were old, the poor sod looked like a tramp, and so they took him to a hospital for poor people. Finally, at the very last minute, a priest recognized him. They always do, don't they. Three days after, he died. A genius or a lunatic. Epic.

Ha, and my mate Georgina, I don't think we were friends when you were at home we only met at Secondary, she saw a photo of his Sagrada Familia and thought she was going to fucking Disney Land! Disney Land, that's just genius, isn't it?! Anyway, my mates all come back saying how they'd had the most amazing time, like, ever? And how they'd gotten pissed with Mr Holdsworth, my art teacher, the one who's obsessed with Bonnard's wife in the bath? Anyway, they'd drunk sangria, and then this authentic Spanish thing, which is red wine mixed with coca-cola. So that's what we were drinking last summer in a field full of crispy-coated cowpats. The usual glamour. We had a fire, there were guitars, we got wasted. I lost my virginity to my friend Dave. Yeah, Little Dave. But he's my mate, it wasn't anything. He can play The Beatles catalogue by ear. We sang the whole of *Rubber Soul.* We shared a tent. It was, curiosity. I mean, we were just kids. And the big surprise is – the incredible thing is – Dave didn't tell anyone. And neither did I until now. And that's weird for teenagers. It is. Believe me.

But unfortunately Georgina didn't fare so well that night. Bit too much wine and cola.

George was only finger-banged, but.

On the Monday when we went back to school it emerged that she is quite – *spacious* – shall we say. And the boy who had fingered her spread it around. Not literally, of course. That'd be *wrong!* The kids still call her 'Five-Fingers Georgina'. Or 'Bucket'. I don't know which is worse. Poor George.

CHRISTIAN: Epic Fail for Georgina.

FRANCES: Tell me about it.

CHRISTIAN: So this summer you're –

FRANCES: I'm keeping my head down. I'm going to do my 'A' Levels.

CHRISTIAN: Have you actually told Mum that?

FRANCES: And after my first term at University I'm going to spunk my student loan on a trip to Barcelona. Have you been?

CHRISTIAN: No.

FRANCES: Well maybe I'll take you.

CHRISTIAN: I'd love that.

CHRISTIAN: Fran.

FRANCES: Yeah?

CHRISTIAN: I missed you. And I've missed so much.

FRANCES: You can't miss an eight year old.

CHRISTIAN: You can.

FRANCES: You probably thought I'd turn out like *them*.

CHRISTIAN: No, no, and I can help, I'll help you. Get out. UCAS applications and so forth.

FRANCES: It's a while before I'm out of this shit-hole. The problem with being the 'late lamb', Christie, is you get to see so far ahead of you.

CHRISTIAN: You've always had your eyes on the door/

FRANCES: What?

CHRISTIAN: I'm sorry I haven't been around, Fran.

FRANCES: You I forgive. I forgive you.

CHRISTIAN: Think he's cooled down yet?

FRANCES: I don't fucking care if he has or no.

CHRISTIAN: You alright, really, Fran?

FRANCES: I'm just peachy, Christie. Shall we go back now? You seen my room yet? It's an epic win. I painted it vermillion. I feel like Beatrice in hell.

FRANCES reaches out a hand, and CHRISTIAN takes it. They leave.

FIVE

Late that same night.

LIAM sits, partially covered by a duvet, on the settee. He strums the guitar absent-mindedly. A floor lamp is on. The door opens slowly. CHRISTIAN enters in his boxer shorts, carrying a bottle of whisky.

LIAM: Alright?

CHRISTIAN: Oh, Jesus!

LIAM: Jesus, sorry now. I'm on your bed/

LIAM jumps up belatedly, putting down the guitar.

CHRISTIAN: No, you're alright.

LIAM: You're still up/I'm not sleeping, I'm gutted about that fire/

CHRISTIAN: Yeah/I'm having a nightcap, you want one?

LIAM: Oh, alright. Yeah. Cheers. *(LIAM gets up, instantly turns and opens a cabinet, pulls out a tumbler.)*

CHRISTIAN: The glasses are in there –

CHRISTIAN folds back the duvet to make room for them both. He pulls some of the duvet over himself. He folds his legs up onto the sofa and puts the guitar gently, but proprietorially, to one side. LIAM passes CHRISTIAN his glass.

LIAM: Cheers mate.

CHRISTIAN pours LIAM a drink and hands it to him.

LIAM: Cheers.

CHRISTIAN: Here, sit.

LIAM hesitantly sits down beside him. He takes a big gulp of the whiskey. CHRISTIAN stares into his own glass. He sets the bottle down on the floor between them.

LIAM: Play do you?

CHRISTIAN: A bit. My Mum taught me.

LIAM: Did she?

CHRISTIAN: Yeah.

LIAM: I never knew she could play.

CHRISTIAN: She's brilliant, yeah.

LIAM: Ha, well I never knew that.

CHRISTIAN: No?

LIAM: Good old Paula. What'd she play in a band?

CHRISTIAN: Nah. Few solo gigs and a demo when she was young. Pubs mostly.

CHRISTIAN: How's your arm?

LIAM: Stings. I'll live.

CHRISTIAN drinks.

A tiny screaming sound is heard.

CHRISTIAN: What was that?

LIAM: Eh?

CHRISTIAN: I heard something.

LIAM: I didn't hear anything/

CHRISTIAN: Shh.

They listen.

LIAM: Owl?

CHRISTIAN: Shh.

They listen.

LIAM: Might be me dog? He kips out/

CHRISTIAN: There!

A tiny screaming sound is heard.

They both look around the room.

CHRISTIAN: It's like a tiny, baby scream. How weird!

LIAM: A tiny scream? Was it?

CHRISTIAN: You heard it?

LIAM: Yeah, but.

CHRISTIAN: Like a Borrower's shut his hand in a door.

LIAM: Could be foxes.

CHRISTIAN: Nah.

LIAM: Got barbed cocks, haven't they.

CHRISTIAN: Have they?

LIAM: Vixens scream blue murder on account of the Man Fox's cock. Same as cats. Evolved with barbs on the cock so's once it's – in – it can't so easily – fall out.

CHRISTIAN: God.

LIAM: It's a miracle the vixens don't all get together and form a posse/

CHRISTIAN: Yeah. *(He laughs.)*

LIAM: But they put up with it. Starting a family's more important. Or something.

CHRISTIAN: Well then I'd be a lesbian vixen.

LIAM: Oh me too, for sure.

They laugh a little. They relax.

CHRISTIAN pours another drink for the two of them.

LIAM: Cheers.

I'm sorry about your room/

CHRISTIAN: Oh that's alright. I'm fine down here. I'd go to a hotel, but/

LIAM: It'd break your mother's heart.

Pause.

CHRISTIAN: And how is it?

LIAM: What's that?

CHRISTIAN: The room. The room okay?

LIAM: Yeah, it's great, it's fine. Thanks.

CHRISTIAN: Sorry you had to be witness, to all that.

LIAM: Oh that? It's family, isn't it?

CHRISTIAN: Is it?

LIAM: Well –

CHRISTIAN: How do you like working for my Dad?

LIAM: Yeah, it's good work. I wanted – you know, to stop moving around, learn a trade. He's been – good to me.

CHRISTIAN: Good. That's good.

LIAM: Yeah.

CHRISTIAN: You were moving around?

LIAM: Yeah. Yeah. Army. I never really settled anywhere before. So.

CHRISTIAN: There's not many thatchers around anymore.

LIAM: No. No, exactly! I'm lucky your Dad could take me on when he did.

CHRISTIAN: Yeah.

LIAM: You never – thought about it yourself?

CHRISTIAN: No. I helped out here. Mum was ill a lot.

LIAM: Paula, she was ill?

CHRISTIAN: Yeah. A bit. Yeah. Years back.

LIAM: And I hear – I heard you're working on the Mill.

CHRISTIAN: Well, I'm working on working on the mill.

LIAM: I heard about that too.

CHRISTIAN: Yeah.

LIAM: You've a meeting tomorrow.

CHRISTIAN: At two. The old man's got himself a place on the Council now, so it's pistols at dawn.

LIAM: Christian –

CHRISTIAN: Yeah?

LIAM: Your Dad, he's had a hard time of it. With your sister.

CHRISTIAN: Oh?

LIAM: It's just an observation.

CHRISTIAN: Yeah. Poor him.

LIAM: She's been jumping up and down waiting for you to come back/

CHRISTIAN: Has she?

LIAM: Yeah/

CHRISTIAN: So she talks to you?

LIAM: Now and then.

CHRISTIAN looks at LIAM steadily.

CHRISTIAN: Well, she's just a kid. She's rebellious.

LIAM is flustered –

LIAM: I've something, there's something I think –

CHRISTIAN: What is it?

LIAM: Tonight – Your Dad, he was driving like merry hell to get back there when we realised what was on/

CHRISTIAN: Yeah/

LIAM: We were flying down the lane back towards the cottage, the brigade were behind us, the smoke was rising, great cloud of it already you could see, but something caught my eye out the window. Coming through a field, cutting through the field – I saw my dog, see.

CHRISTIAN: Your dog.

LIAM: You met him? He's a little fella –

CHRISTIAN: Yeah, yeah –

Pause.

LIAM: Yeah.

CHRISTIAN: Oh *fuck*/

LIAM: We were going like the clappers, but I happened to see out my window. Your sister – Frances – was running back this way, away from the cottage –

CHRISTIAN: You think Fran had something to do –

LIAM: No, no. I don't know.

CHRISTIAN: Oh god.

LIAM: You don't think?

CHRISTIAN: Well, I don't know – what was she doing?

LIAM: Just, running. From that direction. With my dog there.

CHRISTIAN: Fran wouldn't – she wouldn't do that?

LIAM: Well, I thought I'd mention it – I didn't want to mention it before, get a young girl into trouble.

Pause.

But she has a little bit of a history, with – ah, the old pyrotechnics.

CHRISTIAN: Right.

LIAM: I think everyone's thinking it – but not saying it. But what I saw/

CHRISTIAN: Yeah. It points to her.

LIAM: But your Dad – she's not been on speaking terms with him, it seems, for quite some time/

CHRISTIAN: Eight years.

LIAM: Is it?

CHRISTIAN: Apparently. I didn't really register. Mum said whenever I spoke to her, 'Frances still won't speak to your Dad'. I didn't realise she meant literally, not speaking a word.

LIAM: As long as I've been here, she hasn't said a word to him.

CHRISTIAN: Christ.

LIAM: Yeah.

CHRISTIAN: You think maybe she did it to hurt him.

LIAM: Now, I'm not saying she did – I'm just saying – I wasn't sure who – but they said she's close to you, looks up to you, so I thought, go to you first. Come to you with it, see.

CHRISTIAN: Yeah. Thanks – I'll have to talk to her.

LIAM: Right. Good. Good.

CHRISTIAN: Maybe don't mention it –

LIAM: I won't/

CHRISTIAN: To anyone else.

LIAM: No. No.

CHRISTIAN: Cos it's not definite, proof. And he's quick – to jump to conclusions. He's so terrified of losing control that that's exactly what happens.

LIAM: Yeah. I saw.

CHRISTIAN: Yeah, you did.

LIAM: Well, I'd better get to bed.

CHRISTIAN: Right. Okay. Thanks, for telling me about it –

LIAM: It's good to meet you.

CHRISTIAN: Yeah, likewise/

LIAM: I'd built a picture of you, see, from your room. It's a strange thing to sleep in a boyhood room. Stranger still when it's not your own. Makes me think about, the past, you know –

CHRISTIAN: Yeah. They're not ones for redecorating.

LIAM: Oh, no, it's fine. Your Mum there, packed some things into your closet. I like it, the room. I take the top bunk. By the bed, there's a wildlife calendar from 1990.

CHRISTIAN: *(Amused.)* Is there?

LIAM: Yeah.

CHRISTIAN: Well, I give you permission to throw it out.

LIAM: I looked through it.

CHRISTIAN: Anything incriminating on it from that bygone age? Scouts? Dates with girls?

LIAM: Until now I couldn't work out what they were –

CHRISTIAN: They?

LIAM: Yeah –

CHRISTIAN: What?

LIAM: On some of the days you'd drawn a little symbol, a little belt buckle –

CHRISTIAN: A belt –

LIAM: A lot of the days –

Now I see it's a belt buckle.

CHRISTIAN: A belt –

LIAM: God – I'm sorry – I've a big stupid mouth/

CHRISTIAN: No – no. It's okay.

The worst thing is that, the truth is, sometimes – I think I imagined it.

LIAM: Looked real enough to me.

CHRISTIAN: We don't talk about it. So now sometimes I think – I'll see a two-year-old boy, like my friend's kid – and I look at the little boy and think, can my Dad really have hit me, when I was this little, this high? But he did. Didn't he? He's hit me since I was two. It's my first memory.

LIAM: Jesus.

CHRISTIAN: I don't think he was ready for kids.

LIAM becomes nervous.

LIAM: I'm keeping you up.

CHRISTIAN: You believe me.

LIAM: Yeah. I do, course, yeah.

CHRISTIAN: Then can you keep it?

LIAM: What?

CHRISTIAN: – that calendar. Can you just keep it, up there?

LIAM: Yeah. Course. Course I will.

CHRISTIAN: Ok.

LIAM: Ok.

CHRISTIAN: Thanks. Goodnight then.

LIAM takes his glass with him as he gets up.

LIAM: Goodnight.

LIAM exits. CHRISTIAN pulls the duvet around him and surveys the room. He looks as if he's seen a ghost. He covers his eyes with his hands.

SIX

The following day. The day of the meeting.

The Paper Mill in Newtown, beside the rapid flowing river. CHRISTIAN stands looking into the mill pond. FRANCES comes running, she's out of breath. He takes off his yellow hard hat and throws it to her.

FRANCES: *(Catching it.)* I'm not wearing that.

CHRISTIAN: Put it on.

FRANCES: Er – no?

CHRISTIAN: Fran.

FRANCES: Jesus. There's no work going on!

CHRISTIAN: Don't rub it in.

FRANCES puts on the hard hat.

CHRISTIAN: Ah, stunning. You look like one of the Village People.

FRANCES: *Ha* – What's so bloody urgent?

CHRISTIAN: I want to talk to you.

CHRISTIAN surveys the site.

FRANCES: So – we find out in an hour if you're moving in.

CHRISTIAN: Yeah, and with Dad waiting for me, you know what their answer'll be.

FRANCES: Will you pull out? If this one's refused?

CHRISTIAN shrugs.

FRANCES: Just do another one, draft another one, right?

CHRISTIAN: I don't know, Fran. I'm up shit creek if truth be told.

FRANCES: So your job's on the line? Christie –

CHRISTIAN: I'll be fine.

He looks up at the chimney.

CHRISTIAN: The chimney goes obviously.

They stand together, staring up at the mill chimney.

FRANCES: Yeah. It's a motherfucker.

CHRISTIAN: It's one hundred feet tall.

FRANCES: Jesus.

CHRISTIAN: Eight feet in diameter.

FRANCES: Yeah, I wouldn't want that in my garden.

CHRISTIAN: But we'd keep the old forge, that becomes a cottage, build on the lathe house if it holds and it becomes a pair of semi-detached, keep the main pond, but fence it, and keep the side of the mill where the water-wheel is.

FRANCES: Keep all that? What for?

CHRISTIAN: Make a feature of the wheel. It's survived this long. Its shaft's made from a single trunk.

FRANCES: You sound like the old man sometimes.

CHRISTIAN laughs.

CHRISTIAN: I do need to talk to you.

FRANCES: We've eight years' worth to get through, you know.

CHRISTIAN: I had a chat with Liam last night.

FRANCES: What about? Why?

CHRISTIAN: He was still up when everyone was in bed.

FRANCES: And? What did he say?

CHRISTIAN: Well.

FRANCES: What's he said?

CHRISTIAN: He's worried my baby sister's an arsonist.

FRANCES: You what?

CHRISTIAN: You heard me.

FRANCES: What the fuck's that mean? Christie?

CHRISTIAN: He says you were there yesterday, at the fire.

FRANCES: Liam said that?

CHRISTIAN: Yeah. Did you do it?

FRANCES: No I fucking did not! Christ, Christie!

CHRISTIAN: Know who did?

FRANCES: No I don't! How should I know? Why'd he say that?

CHRISTIAN: As I said, you were seen.

FRANCES: I was out walking his bleeding dog, Monsieur Poirot. I didn't do it.

FRANCES: I didn't! Why would I?

CHRISTIAN: I don't know.

FRANCES: Don't be a pleb, Christian.

CHRISTIAN: A what?

FRANCES: I was up that way, but I didn't do it. I didn't even smell any smoke.

CHRISTIAN: Fine.

FRANCES: Alright?

CHRISTIAN: Fine, fine. All I'm saying is, if you did do it, you could tell me.

FRANCES: I didn't do it! What you doing getting all accusatory with me for? You sound like them.

CHRISTIAN: Liam was worried.

FRANCES: Like hell he was.

CHRISTIAN: I think he was worried.

FRANCES: Worried alright. He only thinks of himself. Trying to ingratiate himself into our family and the idiot gets me into trouble! Stinking gypo. Stinking fucking arsehole!

CHRISTIAN: Look, he only told me because he was worried about you.

FRANCES: Yeah right.

CHRISTIAN: And Dad's business.

FRANCES: He doesn't give a shit about the business! He doesn't want to be an apprenticed thatcher any more than you or I. He's using us cos he can't decide what to do with his pathetic life! He's traumatised!

CHRISTIAN: He is?

FRANCES: Like you wouldn't believe. He has these nightmares/

CHRISTIAN: Fran –

FRANCES: Only an idiot signs up to be cannon fodder/

CHRISTIAN: He seems alright to me.

FRANCES: He's used us.

You're not supposed to like him!

CHRISTIAN: I don't dislike him/

FRANCES: I thought you'd hate him!

CHRISTIAN: Why?

FRANCES: Dad's proud as punch to have Liam working for him. Finally he's the boss of someone.

CHRISTIAN: He's the son Dad never had.

FRANCES: Don't say that.

Pause.

CHRISTIAN: Army man. Macho.

FRANCES: Hardly. All he did was twiddle about with fibre optics. And now he's got a guilt complex.

CHRISTIAN: So you didn't do it.

FRANCES: What do you care?

CHRISTIAN: I care – I mean, it's a pretty shit thing to have happened.

FRANCES: A roof pre-dating the chimney, fourteenth century! Ooh! There've been thatchers since the Bronze Age! A water wheel from seventeen eighty-six! Who gives a shit, Christie. Who wants to live here? People like that city couple and the Sunday Drivers just buy up all the country bumpkin shit! Dad there with his bumpkin ways! *(Mocking his accent.)* the 'Master Thatcher'! What do you care whether I did it? I'm fucking stuck here in this backwater and you've escaped!

CHRISTIAN: Of course I care, Fran. It's just if people thought you were setting fire to things – it would not bode well for Dad's business, or for Mum. I mean, it looks dodge that he made the roof and then it burned, a few hours after. There can't be any more, is all I'm saying.

FRANCES: Well he took it out on you anyway! Don't defend him! I've defended *you* for eight years, and you don't give a shit about me! How do you know he never beat me? You ever fucking ask?

CHRISTIAN: He didn't, Fran? Did he? You would have told me? Fuck, Fran – you would have said, on the phone –

FRANCES: No. He didn't. He saved up all his thrashings for you.

Beat.

CHRISTIAN: You haven't spoken to him since I left.

FRANCES shakes her head.

CHRISTIAN: I never expected you to stop *speaking* to him! Bloody hell! Eight years! I don't know anyone that could do that! You were just a kid!

FRANCES: You don't know anything about anything, Christie!

CHRISTIAN: Did I though? I didn't ask you to hate him on my behalf!

FRANCES: You don't know anything!

CHRISTIAN: You don't need to – you didn't need to go *mute* – to exact revenge on my behalf/

FRANCES: Oh wake up, Christie! We all pretended it didn't happen. I was a kid but I remember – everything! Don't you? Don't you remember? If you saw it happening to me, then you'd see how wrong it was.

CHRISTIAN: It's too late, Fran. World's made up of two kinds of people, those who can forgive their parents, and those who can't.

FRANCES: And which are you?

CHRISTIAN: I don't yet know.

FRANCES: Urghh! I *wish* he'd tried to hit me, I would've broken his fucking face! I wish he'd had a go, just *once* – and it's not for wont of trying. I tried everything, to provoke him. And then I hit upon the silent treatment, and you know what, that fucking kills him! Fucking eats him up inside!

CHRISTIAN: Don't cry, Fran, please –

FRANCES: You should try it some time, Christie. Instead of laughing every time he beat you. If you'd just cried, once, he might have stopped! You do know that, don't you? It was the laughing. Laughing at him.

FRANCES: Mum once said Grandda used to beat Dad – so a whole lineage of angry fucking *men* wielding their belts. All the men in our family passing it on! Yes, what a strong family tree we have! Passing it down through the generations!

CHRISTIAN: Well, it stops with me. I'm not having kids.

FRANCES: But if you do?

CHRISTIAN: It'd be a miracle.

FRANCES: But say you did – adopt or get a surrogate or something – if you did have kids, and it was a boy, how do you know you wouldn't hit him? Do you believe it's inherited? No, it's not, I didn't mean it, it doesn't have to/

CHRISTIAN: If I ever had a kid – I couldn't be sure. I'd be terrified of hitting them. Obviously as a preventative measure I'd always wear very tight trousers that don't need a belt. Or dungarees. Or casual tunics.

FRANCES laughs.

FRANCES: It wasn't always just the belt though, was it.

CHRISTIAN: 'Just' the belt? You ever been thwacked with a fucking belt? I'd say the belt was the fucking cream. It was the weapon of choice.

FRANCES: Remember that one time he threw the *Guinness Book of Records* at you, and it knocked your tooth out.

CHRISTIAN: I thought – that was before you were born.

FRANCES: No, it was in the dining room. Your teeth went through your lip, and one of them just stayed there, stuck in your bottom lip there.

CHRISTIAN: Yeah! Oh Christ, that's right!

FRANCES peers at his face closely.

FRANCES: Blood everywhere.

CHRISTIAN: You remember that.

FRANCES: It's all here. *(She points to her head.)* In the Captain's Log.

CHRISTIAN: You didn't have to take revenge for me.

FRANCES: Oh for Christ's sake, Christie! Of course I did!

CHRISTIAN: All these, fires, are they..?

FRANCES removes her hard hat and thumps CHRISTIAN with it.

FRANCES: I won't dignify this!

CHRISTIAN: What about those bus stops.

FRANCES: Jesus!

CHRISTIAN: If you can't trust me, then/

FRANCES: That was a simple case of a rocket mistaken for a Catherine Wheel. It was kid's stuff.

CHRISTIAN: It was more than one bus stop.

FRANCES: Oh for fuck's sake, it was years ago! And when's the last time you saw a bus around here?

CHRISTIAN: The school bus.

FRANCES: That doesn't count.

CHRISTIAN: I just don't want to see you screw up your future over some teenage angst.

FRANCES: Now you're getting patronising.

CHRISTIAN: Sorry. Sorry.

FRANCES: Maybe I've already screwed up.

CHRISTIAN: No, you haven't. You haven't. We'll have a chat about it.

FRANCES: *(Worried.)* What?

CHRISTIAN looks at his watch.

CHRISTIAN: 'A' Levels. And beyond.

FRANCES: – Ok.

CHRISTIAN: I'm going to have to get going. Walk me to the hall?

FRANCES: No I'm going to stay here for a bit. Walk back along the river.

CHRISTIAN: You be alright? Cos I'll lock the gates after me. *(He passes the hard hat to her again.)*

FRANCES: I can go along the river, remember.

CHRISTIAN: Alright. Wish me luck.

He hands her back the hard hat.

FRANCES: Knock 'em dead. Christie –

CHRISTIAN: Yeah?

FRANCES: I didn't do it. It must have been electrical. I wouldn't – there was a family in there, y'know? And I like other people's families.

CHRISTIAN: Alright. I believe you.

CHRISTIAN leaves. FRANCES hugs the hard hat to her chest. She stares up at the mill chimney.

SEVEN

Later that day.

The cottage living room. Early afternoon. PAULA has been watering the money trees on the dining table. She moves around lightly, but there is tension. From time to time she unconsciously, but menacingly, waves a plant-watering atomiser at him. LIAM sits nervously on the settee. From time to time he glances at the door.

PAULA: It was a hot summer and I'd cut a mini-dress from a pattern my sister had and as I drove Bud kept looking down at my lap, my thighs! Out here everything but the fashion and the music passed us by. It all passed me by. We didn't have the choices you had back then – I had to leave school at fifteen, get a job. What was I going to be, anything other than an office junior, with hopes of one day becoming someone's secretary? My eldest brother was the first of the boys to escape, off to the city. God I was jealous of Jack, but the day he left he gave me his guitar. Off he went, and I was stuck here handing over my wages every week to my Dad. My brothers were all moving out one by one, but you couldn't, as a girl. My cousin Susan was always on at me to move in with her in the city, and god I wanted to! She went to all these gigs, met all the bands I was crazy over. She phones me up one day and says her friend's got this bedsit, she's moving out and I could take over the rent. In the city! And I'm a qualified secretary by now. So I applied for a job, and another and another, until finally they said, come in for an interview. And I did! Took the train up on my own and Susan and I had coffee, and I got the job! Only, I was going with Bud then. Talking about getting engaged. So I had two – conflicting – escape routes, see.

But I played that guitar every day, I had it in my head I could be a folk singer if I just wrote some decent songs! I wanted to live, get some life experience, write – Do more gigs, practice, practice and make a demo. That night I drove through Newtown in Bud's mini hatchback. We used to drive down to the river and he'd spread out the blue tarpaulin and we'd lie right by the water. I turned off into the track by the Paper Mill. I pulled the guitar from the backseat. I told him to take the wheel – something we used to do in the old days – a little thing the two of us did when one of us was driving: stupid, dangerous when you think about it now! I told him – I can't forget – I said 'Bud, you steer, take the wheel – I feel a song coming on' and he laughed – I laughed – he leaned over, and steered – and I played a few chords – I thought I had a song, see – and he was watching me – in love with me – and we went off the track, and the car slid down the riverbank, and I only just braked in time to stop us going into the river! He was mad as all hell! We laughed eventually, but we could have gone right in the water!

And that night as we lay on the tarp by the water, Christian was conceived. I held off telling Bud about the job I'd got lined up in the city, and before I knew it I was three months pregnant, and nothing doing – I didn't have a choice, see. I just thought – you had two escape routes, so now you've only got the one, no big deal. And I was happy with it – happy to leave home – start a family of my own –

But all this time Bud seems to blame Christian, I think to myself, it was *me*, it was *that night,* that's when it all changed. I was thinking about *my* escape routes, and I never wondered if Bud had one! Something other than us, staying here, repeating what *our* parents did! And – it's true – I don't have any greater sense of the world than my old Ma did – but I know one thing – I know that a mother gets to see the best years of her children's life and they get to see the worst of hers. But that's how it should be! I wish Bud saw that that's how it should be! I get to see the best years of her life, and she gets to see the worst years of mine!

And what you've just done here Liam, is try to take that from me. Frances hasn't been an easy child to raise, but I still had a chance! And stupid, stupid woman that I am, I didn't put two and two together when the floorboards were creaking up there, but I can't ignore it now, can I? Two months gone! You come to *me*, why? Protection of the Mother hen? Well I'm no good as protection, you see that don't you? I've not protected my children. I've got to start, right now.

You're going to take no responsibility.

LIAM: No Paula – I've said, I could, I mean she's young, but/

PAULA: You're not hearing me, Liam. You're going to leave the way you came in.

LIAM: Paula/

PAULA: Have you heard a word I've said? I've told you my life story, every measly bit of it. I've just confessed to you. Why, Liam? Why do you think I've bothered to tell you?

LIAM: I/

PAULA: Because you're going. Women are getting older nowadays when they have kids. Or they're not having them at all. They're making *decisions!* And I'm damn well going to make sure she makes a decision about this, to hell with Bud/

LIAM: You mean/

PAULA: I'm not going to have her stuck here on account of a grown man who couldn't keep his pants on. As terrible as it may sound to you, I'm going to help her out of this. I've given her Jack's guitar! I'm going to give her every means possible.

LIAM: You're telling me to leave, Paula, that's what you're saying here?

PAULA: What you going to do, live here forever and have a whole tribe of kids under this roof? Turn to drink and beat your children for the brilliant bloody life you think they stole from you?

LIAM: No. I wouldn't/

PAULA: You say that now!

LIAM: I didn't know what to do – I wanted to come to you, but you've decided for her/

PAULA: Because she's still a child! She's a child, so what does that make you? Eh?! You leave now, before Bud gets home. She's my child!

LIAM: Paula/

PAULA: You really want to have this conversation with him?

LIAM: I/

PAULA: Liam. Are you in love with my daughter?

LIAM: I – I don't know.

PAULA: Not a very good way to start, is it?

LIAM: I don't know.

PAULA: You don't know. I'll tell you, Liam. It's not a good way to start. It's not the way this is going to start, without even a bit of love. You better get going. You get out Liam. You get the bloody hell out!

She aims the atomiser at him, about to spray.

A tiny screaming noise is heard. PAULA looks up. She looks out the window.

PAULA: He's got something in his mouth.

She goes closer to the window. She sees something in the back garden.

PAULA: Oi! No. No!

She bangs on the window.

PAULA: Bloody dog! Your bloody dog!

She rushes out of the room. LIAM hurries out after her.

PAULA: *(Off.)* Drop it! Let go! Come here! Oh, no!

You get out of here! You take this bloody dog with you!

The front door opens.

BUD and CHRISTIAN enter. BUD is wearing his wedding suit from scene one.

BUD: Paula?

Paula!

BUD sits on the settee and takes off his shoes. He rubs his feet.

BUD: Oh, that's better.

CHRISTIAN sits down at the other end of the settee.

PAULA enters the room, shaking. Her hands are cupped around a dead frog.

BUD: What the bloody hell you got there?

Paula?

CHRISTIAN gets up and goes to his mother. She opens her hands and shows him the frog.

PAULA: I heard him screaming. A tiny scream! I thought he had a tennis ball in his mouth! But he's dead! That bloody dog's killed my frogs!

BUD laughs.

PAULA: It's not funny, Bud! How'd you find it funny?

CHRISTIAN: The screaming. It was –

PAULA: My frogs.

PAULA strokes the lifeless frog.

BUD: Put it down woman! It's dead! Dog didn't know no better. He's a dog! Put it down, put it outside.

PAULA: I should have seen it coming.

CHRISTIAN: We'll bury him.

PAULA: There's more out there. They've been screaming for days in that bloody dog's mouth and I've been too blind to notice.

BUD: We'll get you some more. We'll grow you some, get some more spawn.

PAULA: They've got the tiniest voices. The tiniest screams I ever heard.

BUD: For god's sake woman! That wont screaming you heard, it was the air coming out of them! It wasn't screaming!

It's the noise of a frog punctured by teeth! It was the air whistling out of them!

PAULA: That's even worse! Oh shut your mouth, Brian Cudden!

CHRISTIAN: Give him here, Mum. I'll bury him.

PAULA: No. *(Defiant.)* No.

PAULA cups the frog gently. She looks down at it for strength. She turns angrily to BUD.

PAULA: Don't you dare sit there looking so bloody pleased with yourself!

BUD: What have I done? Jesus, woman.

PAULA: I can see how the council meeting went from that smug look on your face.

(Stern.) Am I wrong?

BUD: We did reject another application, yes.

PAULA: Oh, I knew it! *(She almost throws the frog.)* And was it you who had the last vote by any chance?

BUD: It was unanimous.

PAULA: You can't stop him! He'll draft another one, a better one, even better/

BUD: But he's not trying again, is he/

PAULA: He will.

BUD: He won't. That's final. Your son's a very gracious loser. Aren't you, Christian?

CHRISTIAN: *(Smirking.)* I'm a very gracious loser.

The front door opens. FRANCES enters the room quietly.

PAULA: He ain't the loser.

BUD: Oh for god's sake woman, put that bloody frog down. It's got enough holes in it to be one of those – china whistles, squat things/

PAULA: An ocarina.

BUD: Ocarina –

PAULA: He had thatch cottages in there, you read that?

BUD: It was mentioned.

PAULA: You even read the bloody thing?

BUD: Thatch wouldn't fit that part of the village.

PAULA: Maybe so, but he was going to throw some work your way!

BUD: I don't want his crumbs! I'm his father, I don't need his bloody charity!

PAULA: Don't you? Don't you Bud? What you think just because Christian's company's pulling out – after four years – that some other developer won't come in?

BUD: Ay, if anyone else wants to throw money away, take a gamble. If the economy turns.

PAULA: Whether it turns or not, you're the one stuck in a dying, a dead, tradition!

BUD: You watch your mouth.

PAULA: Or what? Or what?

BUD: Just leave it, Paula. Leave it! It's over!

PAULA: You should be ashamed of yourself!

BUD: Me?

PAULA: Our son! You're supposed to help him, not ruin him!

CHRISTIAN: I'm not ruined. I'll be alright.

BUD: I'll be here, I'll be waiting if there's a next one. I'm going to fight tooth and nail for that mill to be let alone/

PAULA: Let alone! Let alone! It's been let alone for six years! What you going to do, use your own great personal fortune to re-start it?

BUD: It'll stay closed, not developed. It's a memorial!

PAULA: To what?

BUD: To the men that worked there! The history of the place! Christ, you don't know what you're talking about, shoot your mouth off and you know nothing!

PAULA: They were laid off, Bud. It's not your battle!

BUD: My father and my grandfather worked at that mill/

PAULA: Yes. A hundred years ago when it wasn't cheaper to import the finished product from Russia.

BUD: In their day they were better than the Dutch at making their paper, their paper was high-grade, good enough for money to be printed on!/

PAULA: But the Russians/

BUD: To hell with the Russians! My own father worked seventy-two hours a week as a young lad for seven shillings and sixpence!

CHRISTIAN and FRANCES exchange a look.

BUD: You don't know anything! They were some of the first to make bank notes! *(Lost, nostalgic: he tries to recall the exact routine.)* The place was full of government inspectors making sure no one took any of the watermarked paper, but they trusted my old man. Didn't have to worry about keeping an eye on him. They made the highest-grade currency paper and he never stole a single slip! That mill was one of the finest in the country!

PAULA: And they ended up – making the wrapping paper for the bouquets you get at garages!

BUD: You've got to have respect for craftsmanship! You can't tear down a place like that! A place like that doesn't need a facelift, doesn't need remodelling, it just needs to *remain!* That stream had beautiful clear water and a constant levee of trout in the tail-race below the water wheel! Its shaft's made from a single trunk!

CHRISTIAN: I was going to keep the wheel!

BUD: And now – *now* – the haulage firm that served the mill for longer than your lifetime, they've sold off all their lorries – it's a knock-on effect!

PAULA: Didn't you stop to think how many would be employed to develop those houses?

BUD: The dry quarry's closing next year! How will we recover? You can't see what's happening to the community! It's the little men like Christian that are driving the economy doo-lally with their greed! He's at the wrong end – thinks I'm the little man! Ask yourself that woman, you think he came back to see you! He came back for a quick profit!

PAULA: Well! There's hope yet. With so many men out of work maybe the village could use a casino! Or another bloody pub! Don't look so damn smug, Brian Cudden. You haven't won anything! Your son's a better man than you'll ever be!

Silence.

BUD: Come here woman. Put that bloody frog down.

PAULA addresses the frog.

PAULA: You brought Liam into this house, and look what he's done.

BUD: Dog did it – it's not Liam's fault!. He's a hunting dog!

PAULA: Oh shut up, Bud.

BUD: Not got a soft mouth for hunting, but we'll soon train him to keep away from the pond/

PAULA: *(Exasperated.)* They've gone!

BUD: Who's gone?

PAULA: Liam, and his dog.

BUD: What you mean gone?

PAULA: Gone gone!

BUD: Left? No he hasn't.

PAULA: He's scarpered. Scarpered just this second when he heard you coming.

BUD: Why?

PAULA: Terrified of what you'd do to him!

FRANCES starts towards the door.

BUD: What you mean he's gone? Gone where? What'd I do to him?

PAULA: For that, dear man, you're better off asking your daughter.

BUD: Frances?

FRANCES opens the door and exits.

BUD: Frances!

PAULA: And in case you're not above hitting a pregnant girl, you should know I will kill you with my own bare hands if you so much as lay a finger on her.

BUD: Frances? What the bloody hell you telling me?

PAULA looks at CHRISTIAN.

BUD: What's she done now? What's she done/What's he done to her?

PAULA: Christian –

CHRISTIAN opens the front door, leaves running.

EIGHT

Above – early evening.

The blue tarpaulin-covered, burned frame of the roof of a once-thatched C14th cottage on the outskirts of the village, at Keyneston's Bridge. A ladder rests against the charred roof. On top of the tarpaulin, on top of the burned rafters, besides the chimneystack, sits LIAM. He smokes a cigarette. The dog barks in the shell of the house down below. FRANCES climbs up to sit beside him. She peers down through the rafters.

LIAM: Hey – I'll come down.

FRANCES: No –

LIAM: Well, go careful then.

FRANCES: Was that the kitchen down there?

LIAM: Yeah.

FRANCES: I knew you'd be up here.

LIAM: Yeah?

FRANCES: You old romantic.

LIAM: Thought I might hang about for a bit.

FRANCES: Well don't linger, not with old Happy Fists after you.

LIAM: No, I uh – I'm moving on, Fran.

FRANCES: I know.

LIAM: If that's ok –

FRANCES: No use both of us getting it in the neck –

LIAM: No – he's not going to – Paula won't let him even try. I wouldn't go if I thought you were in – I mean, I want to stick around and make sure you're – ok – but I think I might make things worse? Don't you think? I tried to talk to her, I panicked – and she wouldn't let me – stay –

FRANCES: She gave you a real rollicking.

LIAM: Yeah.

He smiles, shyly.

FRANCES, with emotion, and relief:

FRANCES: Good.

FRANCES: Think they'll be back? This family.

LIAM: Dunno. Who's to say.

Pause.

LIAM: She wants the best for you. Fran.

FRANCES: I know. Because something good's come out of it. I think. But I can't see it yet. And in a perverse way I know I'll use it. I'll write a song about it one day once the band's gone global. *(Laughs.)* I think I'm going to be fine, is that awful?

LIAM: No! Not at all/

FRANCES: That's how we'll leave it. Neatly romanticised, all fodder for my creative endeavours. Not an ounce of guilt. Yes?

LIAM: Yes.

A long pause.

FRANCES: You going home?

LIAM: Guess it's time.

FRANCES: My lot make you realise what a great family you've got?

LIAM: No. No. Believe it or not, I love your family. You'll laugh –

FRANCES:What?

LIAM: I keep thinking about my old man's farm/

FRANCES: Oh don't be a bumpkin, you're an *engineer-*

LIAM: I can't think of anywhere else I'd rather be.

FRANCES: Then – good. Fine.

LIAM: Good.

FRANCES: I'd better go back. Put him off the scent.

LIAM: Oh – ok – Fran –

FRANCES: Got to say goodbye to Ralphie. I think he's chewing up your bag down there.

LIAM: Mind he doesn't follow you.

FRANCES: He won't.

You're going to be all right you know. What's your motto?

LIAM struggles to looks at her, but does. Steadily:

LIAM: "Certa Cito".

FRANCES: Exactly. You're a lucky man, Liam.

FRANCES climbs precariously to the edge.

LIAM: Oh, why's that?

FRANCES: Not every bloke gets to stick his dick in a genius.

LIAM: *(Laughs.)* Let alone impregnate one; I see that as a real coup –

FRANCES: A once in a lifetime opportunity.

LIAM: Get out of here.

FRANCES: Write to me.

FRANCES reaches the ladder and starts to descend.

LIAM: I'll try.

FRANCES: Proper letters that I can tie up in a ribbon. Until I get bored with you.

LIAM: I will.

FRANCES: And write the dreams down, cos I'll want to hear the really freaky ones.

LIAM: *(Laughs.)* All right.

FRANCES: Goodbye Liam.

LIAM: Bye, Fran.

She disappears from view.

NINE

Later.

Evening at the Mill site.

CHRISTIAN stands in the centre of the site staring up at the great chimney. BUD enters. He pauses, then walks to him. He stares up at the chimney.

CHRISTIAN: I thought Fran'd be here.

BUD: Me too. She not, then?

CHRISTIAN: No. *(Seeing him.)* You alright?

BUD: Your mother.

CHRISTIAN: Your lip's bleeding.

BUD: Gave me a bunch of fives.

CHRISTIAN: Fuck, are you kidding?

BUD: Nope. Undercut. Got me under the chin. This tooth here went through me lip.

They both smile.

BUD: I – I reckon I had it coming to me.

I hope you're not thinking of setting fire to the place. Getting your revenge?

CHRISTIAN: Course not.

It had crossed my mind.

BUD: Ha.

CHRISTIAN: Put some petrol drums in the old forge there, throw a match, and it'd be, "Look, Dad, there's smoke in the old chimney again!"

BUD: Ha, yeah!

Pause.

BUD: You uh, you know about your sister, did you?

CHRISTIAN: No, not a clue. You?

BUD: Your Mum wouldn't let me go after him. I – it's not sunk in. Him, gone. The dog – little Ralphie –

CHRISTIAN: Yeah.

BUD: Your mother. She wants Frances to – get rid of it.

CHRISTIAN: Yeah?

BUD: Yeah.

BUD: You think she will?

CHRISTIAN: Who can say?

BUD: I'll kill him. Leaving her to get rid of a baby.

CHRISTIAN: Better that than them running off together. It's not her fault.

BUD: I'm not on the warpath.

CHRISTIAN: No?

BUD: She looks up to you.

CHRISTIAN: Does she?

BUD: Always has.

CHRISTIAN: Oh dear, not exactly a shining example, am I?

BUD: That's not. Not what I meant.

BUD: I don't –

He looks to CHRISTIAN for an answer. CHRISTIAN looks away.

But will you help us with her?

CHRISTIAN: I'll help her.

BUD: But your Mum said about – an Eco town, up North, she said, you might go after?

CHRISTIAN: Yeah.

BUD: Solar panelled roofs, that sort of thing?

CHRISTIAN: Yeah.

BUD: They cost effective, is it?

CHRISTIAN: In the long run, yeah.

BUD: And rain barrels and things, for the loo water?

CHRISTIAN: Yeah, that sort of thing.

BUD: Sounds a bit backwards if you ask me; it's like this organic food lark, now you're paying for them not to use pesticides. I don't know.

CHRISTIAN: Yeah.

BUD: This eco project is the way forward, then, is it?

CHRISTIAN: Yeah, that is, if they keep me on – *(He waves his hand at the mill site.)*

BUD: They won't fire a lad over one project lost?

CHRISTIAN: If there are cuts to be made, well, maybe I've just moved up the list.

A long pause.

BUD, to himself:

BUD: Another unborn child in the house.

CHRISTIAN: What?

BUD: *(Startled.)* If it – goes. Another one. Like the twins.

CHRISTIAN: Yeah. But it's not quite the same, Dad.

BUD: Isn't it?

CHRISTIAN: Fran's just a kid, really.

BUD: Yeah and she's been caught, at sixteen! I'll kill him/

CHRISTIAN: We're looking for *her.*

BUD: She ever tell you – how they were lost? The twins.

CHRISTIAN: Mum?

BUD: Yeah/

CHRISTIAN: No –

BUD: She lost them at eight months, see.

CHRISTIAN: I know *that/*

BUD: My fault. It was my fault.

BUD walks a short distance away. He stops.

CHRISTIAN: How was it your fault?

BUD: This is what – twenty years ago?

CHRISTIAN: Yeah. Yes.

BUD: Yeah – I'd had a bit of drink. I got home and you were still up – and you wanted a bedtime story read.

CHRISTIAN: Yeah?

BUD: And I said no, not tonight, and – you mustn't think your Mum never tried to stop me, she tried, by God she tried – but – I'd had a few – this time, this night, I got past her – I chased you up the stairs to your room, you jumped into the bottom bunk bed, I was coming to give you a little sting on the legs – I was never any good at it, I thought I would be, but – I could never do the voices – I'd had a few jars and she'd followed and got in between us, and that bunk ladder there, and she fell somehow. Well no – I – hit her, I hit your Mum accidentally like, and she fell on the ladder, and her stomach there, her – And – we lost them – both of them – they were boys – they – were boys too –

CHRISTIAN feels nauseous. He doubles over as if suddenly winded, he puts his hands on his knees.

BUD addresses CHRISTIAN's back.

CHRISTIAN: I remember, that night, I do –

BUD: *(Shakily.)* – My old man – he used to take his belt off after dinner, most nights it was for pure game. Other times, he'd take a bar of soap and jam it in your mouth if you cussed. Little things, like. He'd say 'I can cuss, but you, you've had schooling, you know the other words. You don't cuss in my house. You know the other words'. But one day when I was, god – thirteen, or, fourteen – I socked him back. I hit him on the jaw. And, it might have been a lad's punch, but, he never laid a finger on me after that.

CHRISTIAN: *(Still doubled over.)* And what's that – I wasn't man enough cos I didn't fight back?

BUD: No, no, it was me! Every time – when I clouted you it was me – it was me being – a failure. And each time you laughed, you laughed at me! Holding in those tears, you were telling me, I see you. I can see you – failing, Dad I can see you – failing! And I couldn't stop/

CHRISTIAN: Don't –

BUD: I never meant – I lost you – *all* – and your Mum's tummy there – it's never gone down, has it? It's still as if – lost them late in the game, didn't she – and – she's got that reminder out in front of her, the bump –

Pause.

CHRISTIAN: It wasn't just – the belt Dad, It was the – words – you – told me I'd never amount to anything. Said I'd be a dustbin man.

BUD: Say that, did I? Well there's nothing wrong with being a dustman. There's honour – in that –

CHRISTIAN: I came back. I could finally, come back, and even then –

BUD: Christie –

CHRISTIAN: No –

BUD: No, Christie/

CHRISTIAN: No, Dad.

CHRISTIAN does not look at BUD.

BUD addresses the mill chimney:

BUD: The, ah, the night you were conceived – we knew the day exactly of yours, see, because what with your Mum's old Ma and her father keeping her locked up, it was never easy to get a date – so we knew, when we found out she was pregnant, that it was this one night, down here. Your Mum was a crazy little thing, used to play the guitar while she was driving! And that evening, she was in this dress her Ma had made her, only she'd upped the hem, god she was a looker your Mum! Still is! I used to let her drive and play the guitar along these back roads, look – it wasn't so dangerous back then – and anyway she had the most beautiful voice, god, if she'd kept going, she should have been a singer, a famous one – she was writing one that night, down here. I've got to ask her if she remembers the tune, because, every time I look at you I hear it. Not the words, them I forget, but the tune. I heard it when we came through the door all black from the fire. And I saw you, standing there. Looking like your Grandda Ward. And suddenly I hear that tune. *(He hums a little.)* She would have been famous, Christian, off a song like this. I have to ask her, if she remembers it. I don't do it justice. Christian –

We'll be getting back shall we?

See if she's come home?

You're cold there, Christie. You're cold, son.

What can I do?

CHRISTIAN stands looking up at the chimney, his face impassive.
BUD stands a little ways away from him. He doesn't take his eyes
off CHRISTIAN. They remain like this.

TEN

The living room. FRANCES enters quietly. PAULA and the guitar sit
side-by-side on the sofa. PAULA stands.

PAULA: There you are. You alright?

FRANCES: Yeah. Yeah. I saw Liam off.

PAULA: Has he gone?

FRANCES: Yeah.

PAULA: Well it's for the best.

FRANCES: Is it?

PAULA: Isn't it? You want to throw your life away and stay
here with me for a lifelong babysitter, fine. You decide.

FRANCES: What's with your hand there? Has he –

PAULA: I gave him an upper-cut. I think it was.

FRANCES: Did he swipe you? Mum?

PAULA: No. No he didn't. I did it voluntarily. I took a stand.
And Christ almighty, hitting hurts!

FRANCES: What did he say?

PAULA: Not much. He's gone out to cool down. Pub, probably.
And your brother's out looking for you.

FRANCES: I want to light the biggest fucking fire you've
ever seen. I want to light that water wheel – I want
to light it up like a Catherine wheel, I want some big
fucking explosions! He could have helped him push that
application through, but he's sick, Mum! You don't have to
put up with it! We can go away, Mum, we can go/

PAULA: I've just been on the phone to Martha and she's
getting me a till job. I've not told him yet, I shall look
forward to it. You know what? I'll take anything. Anything
for a bit of my own money.

FRANCES: He'll never let you.

PAULA: Oh he will.

FRANCES: You'll not leave him?

PAULA: You think I'm weak, Frances, but.

FRANCES: After everything he's done –

PAULA: I made my bed, love.

You know, there's a phrase my Ma always said, it's, 'Mad as a box of frogs'. You know, "Cousin Jackie's as mad as a box of frogs". When I lost your brothers, miscarried, well I'm certain she said it about me then! I couldn't go out – they gave me valium, did you know that? I struggled, love, for years with that – I'd leave my shopping, paid for, at the till, 'cause I'd have a little panic and just have to go home – and sometimes, at the school gates, I'd not be able to stand with the other Mums, I'd stand a little ways up the road until I saw Christie and then I'd march him home!… and I thought, over the years, I've gotten better. I came off the pills when I found out I was pregnant with you, and you coming along just made everything better…but what worked best, do you know, what really made me feel better, was when Christie stayed away. Eight years. And I thought, I feel good – because someone is finally punishing me. Of course, it was mostly your father he was staying away from, but I felt good, I felt that was *right*. And deep down, Frances, I felt it was right what you were doing – not the fires, but the – not speaking to him. Each of us, doing our penance. Isn't that a terrible thing to say? Well I've got a full box of frogs again now! I'm mad as hell about all this, I am. But when I say mad, mad, I really mean angry. I'm angry as hell about this family! I'm angry as hell that you've both got a father who thinks with his fists. And god it felt good to hit him, dear god, I see how it's addictive!

Beat.

I went out with the torch just now and collected them up. Eleven little dead frogs I've got in that box. All of them punctured. I'm going to give them a proper burial. You know, like we did when you were little, tissues in a shoe-box, lollipop sticks for crosses, a little Calvary out by the coal bunker. I'm at my wit's end, love. I thought I was going to have a breakdown tonight/

FRANCES: Mum/

PAULA: I did, I'm sorry, I did – I'm sorry – a Mother should never say these things, but I've never been, with my nerves – but once I got all those frogs in the box, I looked down at them, I remembered my Ma's saying, and I almost laughed. I'm not 'mad', I'm angry! And once I've buried them, that's it. We'll deal with this. Pat the earth down, and Peace. Peace from here on out.

FRANCES: I'm getting rid of it.

PAULA turns to look at FRANCES, she studies her. She nods solemnly.

PAULA: I was thinking, I've not had a pay cheque in years. I was thinking, with my first pay cheque you and me, we're going to Spain. How'd that be?

FRANCES: You'd have to get a passport.

PAULA: We'll get you sorted out, and then, we'll go. To hell with the rent.

FRANCES: Alright.

PAULA: We could ask Christie, if he wanted to come.

PAULA picks up the guitar. She sits on the sofa. FRANCES sits beside her. She sits as close to her as she can.

FRANCES: Good. Alright. Epic Win.

Pause.

Written us a song then, have you?

FRANCES picks up a pad and pen from the floor. The pad is scrawled with the notation of a song.

PAULA: It's a very old tune. It's not hip-hop.

FRANCES: Teach it to me.

PAULA: Don't laugh at me.

FRANCES: *You're* not funny.

PAULA: You can change the words.

FRANCES: Why, what's it sung in, Latin?

> *PAULA, composed, plays a few bars. The front door opens. FRANCES stands up expectantly. BUD and CHRISTIAN enter, slowly, but regaining their breath. PAULA stops playing.*
>
> *BUD raises a finger to his lips as if to halt any potential questions. FRANCES watches them intently. CHRISTIAN stands to one side. He looks uncertain, nervous. BUD closes the door quietly and leans against it. He rubs his hands on his old suit trousers. Evenly:*

BUD: It's coming. The mill's on fire.

> *The family regard one another. Only FRANCES smiles, elated – PAULA remains sitting, impassive, without putting down the guitar. CHRISTIAN passes a hand over his face, rubbing his forehead. BUD continues to lean against the door. He looks searchingly to each of them.*
>
> *The End.*